THE QUE[EN] WHO SAVED HER PEOPLE

Book of Esther FOR CHILDREN

Illustrated by Jack Glover

Written by Carol Greene

ARCH Books

Copyright © 1973 by Concordia Publishing House, St. Louis, Missouri

Concordia Publishing House Ltd., London, E. C. 1

Manufactured in the United States of America

All Rights Reserved

ISBN 0-570-06075-3

In long-ago Persia, a land like a dream,
King Ahasuerus decreed that the cream
of all the young maidens be brought to his throne,
and from them he promised to choose one alone.
She'd reign as his queen, and she'd be his dear wife.
(What girl wouldn't love to live that sort of life?)

A kind Jewish servant called Mordecai peered
at the young girls arriving and stroked his long
   beard.
"From far and from near they have come by the
   dozen,
but none are so lovely as Esther, my cousin.

"I'll take her to Ahasuerus' hall,
and if it's God's will, he'll choose her over all."

The folk in the palace all loved Esther dearly,
and soon came the day when the king announced
   clearly,
"It's Esther I've chosen above all the rest."
"Hurrah!" cried the crowd. "He has chosen the
   best!"

The whole kingdom stopped work to honor their queen
with feasts such as never before had been seen.

At first life was sweet for the happy young bride.
Then Haman, a prince who was puffed up with
    pride,
in some sneaky way got the king to decree:
"Now Haman's head servant; to him bend your
    knee!"

The other poor servants just had to obey,
and Mordecai stroked his long beard with dismay,

"Jews bow to their God," said the gentle old man.
"Bow down before Haman? There's no way I can!"

When Haman found this out, he narrowed his eyes
and ran to the king with a whole pack of lies.
The king, all befuddled, at last said, "Okay!
You're head servant, Haman. We'll do it your way."
And what was the terrible thing Haman planned?
To kill every Jew in the whole Persian land!

Now tears of despair flowed from Mordecai's eyes.
Each street that he wandered was filled with his
cries.
It seemed from such evil could never come good.
Then God's Spirit touched him, and he understood:

Queen Esther was Jewish! God gave her that throne so her people would not face their trouble alone.

A servant told Esther about Haman's plan.
"Oh, no!" cried the queen. "What a horrible man!
I'll stop him, I promise! I know what I'll do:
Have a feast for the king and invite Haman too.
And when the king's happy, his tummy quite full,
I'll tell him the trick Haman thought he could pull."

The feast was soon ready, the candles burned
   bright,
but Esther somehow felt the time was not right.
"I'll have them tomorrow to another great feast
And *then* tell the king that his servant's a beast."

So next day the cooks did the whole thing again.
The queen and her guests ate and ate and ate. Then,

"I've something to ask you, dear Ahasuerus,"
said Esther. "Is there any chance that you'll spare
  us?
Would you have your queen killed and her people
  too?

I thought that you loved me. Please tell me you do!"
At first the king thought she was just having fun.
But then Esther told him what Haman had done.

"He *what*?!" cried the king, and did Haman shake
    then,
and soon no one saw him, not ever again.

Good Mordecai took over Haman's old job.
He wisely and happily ruled the whole mob
of servants, who now liked to cook and to clean.
"Our life's so much better. It's thanks to the queen!"

Then all of the Jews in the whole Persian land
held a thanksgiving feast; 'twas the first ever
   planned.
"We thank God for Esther. To Him we sing praise!

"We'll thank Him and trust Him the rest of our
    days."
And Jews to this day every year read the tale
of Esther, who showed them God's love will not
    fail.

DEAR PARENTS:

The story of Esther has several lessons to teach us. One is that anti-Semitism is as old as the Jewish people. You might use the story as a springboard to discuss this specific prejudice and prejudice in general with the child. Point out that the Jewish people are God's Old Testament people whom He loved—and loves—very much.

Present-day Jews do not accept Jesus as their Savior. But that is no reason to hate and persecute them. Rather we should love them and lovingly share our faith with them. We can learn from them too about the feast of Purim, for example, which recalls Queen Esther's victory and which Jews celebrate every year in late winter.

There's another theme running through Esther's story, the powerful theme of trust that dominates the Old Testament and is fulfilled in the New. Help the child realize ways in which God has been faithful to his trust too.

Finally, there is the theme of thanksgiving. The Jews' celebration of their release from Haman's persecution seemed to be almost a spontaneous thing, a great sense of relief and an outpouring of praise to the God, who delivered them. We too have cause for such relief and praise, for through His Son God has delivered us from the worst persecution of all—that of sin and death. What a reason to celebrate!

THE EDITOR